JAN 0 6 2012

# EXTREME IN-LINE SKATING

TAMRA B. ORR

**Marshall Cavendish**
Benchmark
New York

NOTE FROM THE PUBLISHER:
Some in-line skaters have chosen at times not to wear safety gear. Do not attempt this sport without proper gear and taking safety precautions.

This publication represents the opinions and views of the author based on Wil Mara's personal experience, knowledge, and research. The information in this book serves as a general guide only. The author and publisher have used their best efforts in preparing this book and disclaim liability rising directly and indirectly from the use and application of this book.

Other Marshall Cavendish Offices:

Marshall Cavendish International (Asia) Private Limited, 1 New Industrial Road, Singapore 536196 • Marshall Cavendish International (Thailand) Co Ltd. 253 Asoke, 12th Flr, Sukhumvit 21 Road, Klongtoey Nua, Wattana, Bangkok 10110, Thailand • Marshall Cavendish (Malaysia) Sdn Bhd, Times Subang, Lot 46, Subang Hi-Tech Industrial Park, Batu Tiga, 40000 Shah Alam, Selangor Darul Ehsan, Malaysia

Marshall Cavendish is a trademark of Times Publishing Limited

All websites were available and accurate when this book was sent to press.

LIBRARY OF CONGRESS CATALOGING-IN-PUBLICATION DATA
Orr, Tamra.
Extreme in-line skating / Tamra B. Orr
p. cm. — (Sports on the edge!)
Includes bibliographical references and index.
Summary: "Explores the sport of extreme in-line skating"—Provided by publisher.
ISBN 978-1-60870-225-1 (print) ISBN 978-1-60870-746-1 (ebook)
1. In-line skating—Juvenile literature. 2. Extreme sports—Juvenile literature. I. Title.
GV859.73.O77 2012
796.21—dc22
2010016867

EDITOR: Christine Florie   PUBLISHER: Michelle Bisson
ART DIRECTOR: Anahid Hamparian   SERIES DESIGNER: Kristen Branch
EXPERT READER: Justin Eisinger, Editorial Director, *One* Rollerblading Magazine

Photo research by Marybeth Kavanagh

Cover photo by Greer & Associates, Inc./SuperStock
The photographs in this book are used by permission and through the courtesy of: *The Image Works*: Syracuse Newspapers/R. Anglin, 4; Bill Bachmann, 40; *Alamy*: INTERFOTO, 6L; imagebroker, 6R; Janine Wiedel Photolibrary, 9; *Getty Images*: Robert Beck/Sports Illustrated, 10; Romilly Lockyer/The Image Bank, 42; *PhotoEdit*: David Young-Wolff, 15, 20; Michael Newman, 21, 23; *SuperStock*: Westend61, 16; Cusp, 31; Greer & Associates, Inc., 41; *Corbis*: Creasource, 26; Duomo, 33; *age fotostock*: Bjorn Svensson, 29; *AP Photo*: Mark J. Terrill, 34; Tony Gutierrez, 36

Printed in Malaysia (T)
1 3 5 6 4 2

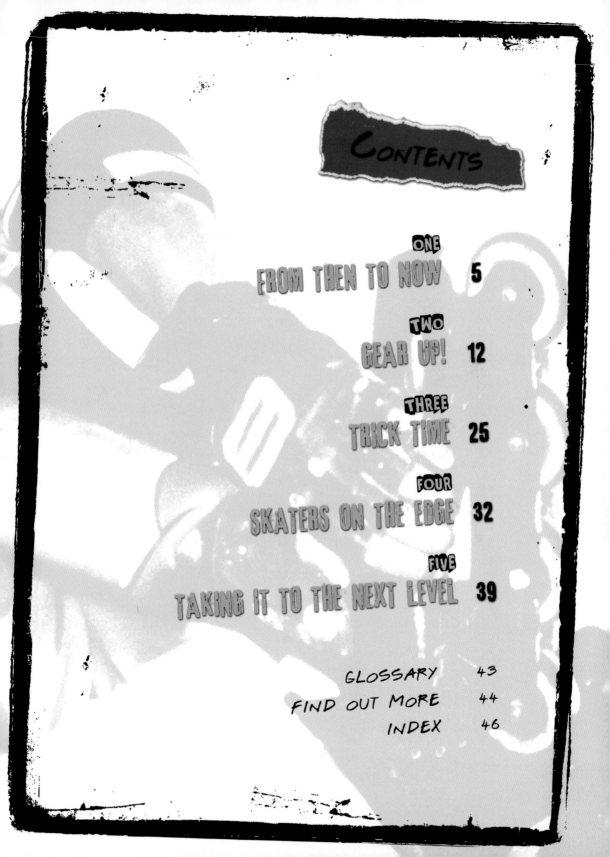

# CONTENTS

# ONE

# FROM THEN TO NOW

**YOU'VE PROBABLY SEEN** the old movies. You may have gone to the roller rink when you were younger. You might even own a pair of sneakers with built-in wheels underneath. Most people recognize roller skates, since these sets of wheels have been around for decades (actually centuries!). However, have you ever seen someone zipping by on a different set of skates? These are sleek. They have aluminum

← IN-LINE SKATING HAS BECOME ONE OF THE MOST POPULAR SPORTS IN THE UNITED STATES. FROM RACING (LEFT), TO FREESTYLE, TO ROLLER HOCKEY, IN-LINE SKATING IS A HEART-PUMPING SPORT!

ROLLER SKATES HAVE COME A LONG WAY. DURING THE EARLY 1900S SKATING WAS A "GENTLER" PASTIME. TODAY, IT HAS TAKEN A MORE HARD–EDGED APPROACH.

or fiberglass frames and wheels made out of tough synthetic materials like nylon or **polyurethane**. The wheels are lined up from front to back almost like an ice-skating blade, instead of the traditional design of two rows of two wheels each. The new models seem to go faster—and skaters do amazing tricks and stunts on them. These are in-line skates, and they are not your grandparents' roller skates by any means!

# A New Kind of Skate

Roller skates were showing their age. In 1966 rebels from the Chicago Roller Skate Company decided to go for a different look and lined up four wheels in a row along the bottom of each skate. Was the invention a hit? Not even close. Fast forward to 1979. Ice hockey players Scott and Brennan Olson were checking out skates in a sporting goods store in Minnesota when they came across a pair of the Chicago Company's unusual roller skates. The brothers realized that skates with wheels would allow them to practice their ice hockey moves on any smooth surface—they wouldn't need a rink, or even ice!

Of course, the store-bought skates were not exactly what the Olson brothers needed, so they started customizing them. They put rubber brakes on the heel and used polyurethane to make the wheels stronger and harder. They added padding to the boots to make them more comfortable. Soon, the Olsons were making pairs for their friends, and before long the two-man enterprise had become a corporation: Rollerblade Inc.®. By the time Scott and Brennan

Olson sold the company in 1985, in-line skating was a billion-dollar business, and people all over the world were hitting rinks, parks, and sidewalks with these skates on their feet.

## Aggressive In-Line Skating Takes Hold

Even the Olsons could not have predicted what would happen to skates in the next generation. Where once the skates were used for simple exercising in the park, by the early 1990s a brand-new passion had taken hold—aggressive or freestyle in-line skating. People still chose to put on their in-line skates and go for a nice spin, but more and more others chose to take their skating beyond that. They started jumping on railings, riding down stairs, flipping over benches and spinning across ramps, leaving the ground and catching air as they went. They invented tricks, shared tips, practiced moves, and started competing. By 1991 the International Inline Skating Association was established. Skating magazines and clubs popped

SKATING DOWN HANDRAILS IS A FORM OF FREESTYLE IN-LINE SKATING THAT ACHIEVED GREAT POPULARITY IN THE EARLY 1990s.

up across the country. A new jargon hit the streets as **street skating** and **vert skating** attracted millions of people.

Today, there are hundreds of skate parks across the United States, mostly in larger cities. In Denver, Colorado, a 60,000–square-foot-park brings young people in from all over the city. Atlantic Beach, Florida, has SkateLab, an indoor/outdoor course where skaters can jump and soar in all kinds of weather, and

A SKATER TAKES ON SOME VERT ACTION DURING THE 1997 X GAMES.

California's Lake Cunningham Regional Skate Park features a 70-foot-long, 22-foot-wide full pipe! Competitions such as the Gravity Games and the X Games featured death-defying skaters who kept the audience gasping with the latest tricks. The "I Match Your Trick Association" created the first-ever true street contest outside the San Francisco X Games, a format since adopted by all other action sports.

Thousands of fans have signed petitions in the hope of adding aggressive in-line skating to the Summer Olympics.

What does this extreme sport require? First, you must have a sense of adventure and a willingness to explore a relatively new field. Next? You must know how to skate, have a good sense of balance, and develop strong muscles. As you practice, all the needed skills will get better, but having these basics will make progress easier and faster. Time to gear up!

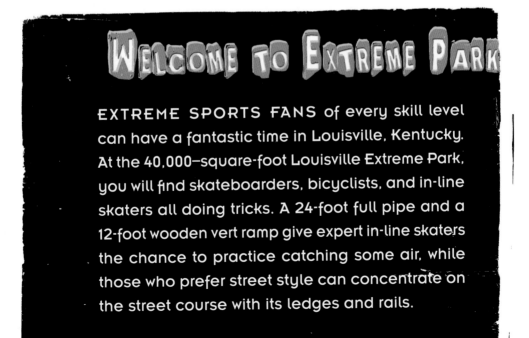

## WELCOME TO EXTREME PARK

**EXTREME SPORTS FANS** of every skill level can have a fantastic time in Louisville, Kentucky. At the 40,000–square-foot Louisville Extreme Park, you will find skateboarders, bicyclists, and in-line skaters all doing tricks. A 24-foot full pipe and a 12-foot wooden vert ramp give expert in-line skaters the chance to practice catching some air, while those who prefer street style can concentrate on the street course with its ledges and rails.

# TWO

# GEAR UP!

**YOU CAN SKATE.** You have balance. You are ready to hit the road or the park, right? Wrong. Going in-line skating before you learn basic moves and putting on the right equipment is both irresponsible and dangerous. You're eager to get started, but make sure to use your brain first, body second.

Believe it or not, the most important step to becoming a great aggressive skater is learning how to fall. You may think that falling is the main thing you want to avoid; but knowing how to do it properly—because you will absolutely, positively fall—often—is the key to not getting hurt and getting back up again.

## Staying Safe

Before we discuss tumbling to the ground, let's explore the gear you will need. A tumble without "armor," as the pros call it, hurts more and heals more slowly. Sure, you need the right skates and boots, but before you use those, you will need to be protected against "road rash" (cuts and bruises) and "raspberries" (scrapes). Like skates and boots, protective gear can be found at skate shops and sporting goods stores.

Of all the parts of your body to protect, your head is the most important. If it gets hurt, nothing else is likely to work right. It is the part of you that is in control of everything else. Be sure to get a helmet rated for multiple impact resistance. Although some skaters used bicycle helmets in the past, today most safety organizations recommend dual-certified helmets, that is, headgear that has been certified for both skateboard and bicycle use.

Next to your helmet, wrist guards are the most important protective equipment you can wear. As you will soon see, they play an important part in the falling process. When you take a spill, your first reaction is to put your arms out. Since wrists tend to take the brunt of the impact, keeping them protected is essential. Wrist guards, which wrap around the vulnerable wrists, are made with metal or plastic pieces inside to keep bones safe. This hard material helps you slide when falling, reducing road rash on your arms, which never feels good.

Two of the most likely areas to crash and burn on asphalt are your elbows and knees. These joints are also at high risk for breaks, strains, and sprains, so wearing thick pads can soften any possible encounters with the ground. More advanced skaters move away from knee and elbow guards and prefer wrist and shin guards.

If you've ever worn shoes that don't fit properly, you know how uncomfortable they can be. Shoes that are too big slip and slide, and shoes that are too small chafe and cause blisters. These problems are even worse with poorly fitting skate boots. Trying to do tricks can be torture if your skates don't fit right. Don't borrow your friend's skates; don't buy a pair that

ONE OF THE MOST IMPORTANT THINGS TO DO BEFORE SKATING IS GETTING PROTECTIVE GEAR SUCH AS A HELMET, KNEE AND ELBOW PADS, AND WRIST GUARDS.

hasn't been personally fitted to your foot. Without properly fitting boots, you will learn more slowly and fall more often. You will also be more likely to get hurt. To find out what size you wear and what type you prefer (hard plastic or leather), you can either rent a pair to try out or spend time at a skate store trying on different models and styles. Keep in mind that like

IN-LINE SKATES MUST FIT YOUR FOOT PROPERLY. CHOOSE THE RIGHT BOOT FOR YOU.

shoes, skates will break in and get slightly roomier. They never get tighter.

Although you don't need to disassemble a boot to know whether it will fit, an understanding of how skates are made can be helpful. In modern in-line skates, a metal, nylon, or fiberglass frame connects the boot to the wheels. The center of the wheel is the **hub**, which contains **bearings**. The bearings are protected with a bearing spacer. Most skates have four wheels, although some racing models have five or six for increased speed.

Wheels come in different sizes as well as different hardness. The smaller the wheel, the more balance you will have. The hardness of the wheels is measured by means of a device called a **durometer**. The higher the number shown on the durometer, the harder the wheel.

# THE INTERNATIONAL INLINE SKATING ASSOCIATION'S RULES OF THE ROAD

**THE INTERNATIONAL INLINE SKATING ASSOCIATION** has established a set of rules for safe skating. Called SLAP for short, they are:

**SMART:** wear your safety gear and keep it in good working order; know the basics of skating

**LEGAL:** know traffic regulations and follow them

**ALERT:** always pay close attention to traffic, safety hazards, and obstacles

**POLITE:** yield to pedestrians; skate on the right and pass on the left

## SKATE CHANGES

As in-line skating has gotten more popular, the demand for better skates has grown. A variety of companies are constantly trying to find ways to make improvements to their models. Recent changes have included sweat-resistant boot liners; thicker, softer cuffs; and flexible bamboo frames that are better able to withstand and absorb road vibration. Increased amounts of the plastic compound urethane have been added to wheels to give them better traction and a longer life. Skates may include soul plates, grind frames, and other special modifications.

Aggressive skaters tend to choose wheels that are rated between 85A and 90A. Wheels for specialized moves like grinding are rated above 101A.

## TIME TO FALL!

Learning to fall is the best way to make sure that when you fall—and you will—you will do it safely. Here are the steps to follow:

1. Put on all your safety equipment.

2. Stand on grass or carpeting so you won't roll.
3. Bend forward at the waist and bring your arms down in front of you.
4. Bend your knees until you cannot see your toes.
5. Reach to touch your knee guards.
6. Keep your head up.
7. Continue bending forward until you start to fall over.
8. As you go down, keep your hands up and fall onto your wrist guards. As you land, slide your hands forward so that your weight is distributed equally between your wrists and your knees.

Practice these moves over and over until you are comfortable with falling and the sequence feels natural.

## Heading Out

You know how to skate. You have your equipment. You've learned how to fall. Is it time to hit the

BELIEVE IT OR NOT, YOU NEED TO LEARN THE PROPER WAY TO FALL. WHAT HAS THIS GIRL DONE WRONG?

pavement? Certainly—but you still need to learn a few basic moves, plus one of the most vital skills of all: how to brake.

According to skating associations, taking in-line lessons from a qualified instructor is one of the best ways to prevent injury. Only 11 percent of the people who are hurt when skating have had six lessons or more. The International Inline Skating Association offers certified instructors, and the National Skate

Patrol is made up of volunteers who help new skaters learn how to skate safely.

When you start, find a smooth, even, obstacle-free surface. An empty parking lot is a good choice; or you could use a rink or a large room with a wooden floor. Before beginning, check for potholes, trash, or anything else that could cause you to fall.

The starting position for in-line skating is simple:

AN EMPTY PARKING LOT PROVIDES A GOOD PLACE TO PRACTICE IN-LINE SKATING.

1. Bend your knees until you can no longer see your toes.
2. Put your feet shoulder width apart, in a *V* position (heels in, toes out).
3. Bend your arms slightly with hands extended, palms facing down.

4. Be as relaxed as possible and look straight ahead.
5. Step forward with your right foot and push with your left to glide forward. Reverse to continue.

This is a basic stride. Practice it until it feels natural and comfortable. To help pick up speed, choose a slight downhill to skate across.

Next, strengthen your leg muscles and increase flexibility by practicing the **lunge**.

1. At first, lean into a wall or hang onto a railing. Later, as you learn how to do lunges, you will not need this support.
2. Keep your skates parallel and bend your knees.
3. Roll your right leg out and behind you, placing your balance on the left foot.
4. Line up your knee over your toes and your chest over your knee. Bend deeper.
5. Repeat, extending your left leg and

balancing on your
right foot.

6. Once you are
comfortable
with this move,
begin gliding and
lunging as you go.

Ready to roll? No!
You haven't learned how

THE BASIC WAY TO STOP WHEN IN-LINE SKATING IS TO DRAG THE RUBBER BRAKE ALONG THE GROUND.

to stop yet. Moving forward is great, but you need
to know how to stop other than by falling down or
running into a wall. There are several methods. Each
person has a preference, so you will develop yours.
Here is the most basic way to brake:

1. Roll your braking skate forward so the heel
   of it passes the toe of your other skate.
2. Next, raise the toe of your braking skate
   until you feel the heel brake's rubber
   dragging on the surface.

3. Finally, aim your hips at the ground and sink into a squat with 90 percent of your weight on the brake. You will come to a complete stop.

This is the heel stop. The T-stop is another choice. In this style, you lunge forward onto one skate and put the other behind you. The dragging of the trailing skate will slow you down. Then, as you pull the trailing skate in, you will come to a stop. If you are skating backward, neither the basic method nor the T-stop will work. Instead, bend your knees deeply and extend your stopping skate behind you, then lower the wheel to the ground and tilt out to stop.

Finally—you know the basic moves and you have been practicing until you can do them naturally. Now, it is time to learn the tricks that put the "extreme" in extreme in-line skating!

# THREE
# TRICK TIME

**NOW LET'S PUMP UP** the action with some hardcore tricks! In this chapter, we explore how to do some skaters' favorite moves, including stalls, grinds, stair bashing, and vert tricks. Each one of these moves is awesome—when you do it right. But remember that as you are learning, you will miss your mark, stumble, fall, and crash.

## STALLS AND GRINDS

One of the most basic street moves is called the stall. You need to know how to do this before you can learn to grind. The stall is all about balance and poise.

Begin by choosing an obstacle and then skate toward it. Jump onto it and aim to lock onto it with the space between your second and third wheels. Hold the position and then jump off.

Once you have mastered the stall, you can add in the grind. In this move you aren't using your wheels at all. Instead, you slide sideways on the frames or boot. There are several kinds of grinds. The most basic are the frontside and backside grinds. In a frontside grind you jump up on a railing, locking it between your skates' second and third wheels, and slide down. The backside is almost exactly the same, only your back is to the rail.

Another common grind is known as the soul grind.

AN EXPERIENCED SKATER GRINDS ON A HANDRAIL.

You jump on a rail, curb, or ledge and then slide on the outside edge of the sole of one skate. Most of your weight is on the sole foot, while the other foot is turned sideways, locked onto the rail between the second and third wheels and supporting about 20 percent of your weight. Other grinds, called royals, full torques, fast slides, acid grinds, alley-oop souls, and x-grind, can be done in many variations and combinations.

## STAIR BASHING AND VERT STUNTS

The very first in-line tricks may have been done by people going down concrete or wooden steps on their skates. When you try stair bashing, start with just a few steps until you gain confidence and experience. Build up speed first so that when you get to the top step, you are going really fast. As you go down the stairs, your knees should be bent, with one skate about 6 inches in front of the other. If you go down the steps forward, you will need to take off your brakes or they will bounce on the steps. Allow your feet to float over the stairs, and keep your ankles relaxed and loose. It is easier to go down stairs backward, but be sure to look behind you so you don't run into anything.

Vertical tricks are those that send you vertical— you're ignoring gravity and throwing yourself up to catch as much air as you possibly can. To get high enough to do this, you have to use wooden or concrete **ramps** like those found in skate parks. Most ramps are between 8 and 12 feet high and made out of quarter-pipes or half-pipes. In a quarter-pipe, a curved wall called a **transition** is attached to a flat surface, known as a **flat**. In a half-pipe, there are two curved walls. As a beginner, start at the bottom of the pipe and then start skating back and forth, building up speed. Push and throw your arms forward to gain power. Slowly start making your way up the side of the wall. Keep your feet together across the flat, and stagger them on the transitions. Feel how your body and balance adjust to the speed and ramp.

As you speed up, you will eventually go vertical. Don't attempt to catch air without a plan on how to land, however. What goes up does come down—and coming down can be hard and painful. Know your abilities.

While you are in the air, you can do some flips (somersaults in the air), spins (from a 180, or half rotation, to a 720, or two full rotations), or grabs (reaching out and grabbing your skates or wheels in different positions). At the top of each wall is a metal railing called a **coping**. Some professional skaters use it to do grinds, which in vert skating lingo are known as **lip tricks**. Skaters who stand at the top of the wall and then jump down call the move "dropping in." It is a good skill to practice because you can't skate a ramp or at a skate park without learning how to do it.

All these moves are likely to feel very hard—and rather scary—when you first attempt them.

WHILE CATCHING AIR, A SKATER PREFORMS A GRAB.

# LEARNING THE LINGO

BIO  spinning around while going off axis

BRAINLESS  aptly named because it is
a 540-degree spin performed while
backflipping

CAMEL TAP  quickly tapping your wheels to the
top of the ramp before reentering the ramp

CESS SLIDE  sliding on the side of your skate
boots across a surface not intended for
grinding

FAKIE  skating backward

FARSIDE  jumping over a rail or ledge to land
and grinding down the opposite side

Here are a few more terms to learn so that you sound
like a pro.

MISTY FLIP  one of the hardest tricks—
spinning 540 degrees off axis (one and
a half turns) and landing backward

MUTE AIR  while in the air, reach in front
and grab the opposite skate with your
hand over the laces or toe

ZERO SPIN  launching backward and
landing backward without spinning

THESE TWO SKATERS DROP IN BY JUMPING DOWN A HALF-PIPE.

Remember to be patient because it takes time and practice to learn in-line skating tricks. It also takes a lot of mistakes, but each one will bring you closer to being able to do the trick. Hang in there!

# SKATERS ON THE EDGE

**LIKE EVERY SPORT,** aggressive in-line skating has its heroes. You know the ones—they make the sport look as easy as breathing. They create amazing new moves. Their skates seem like an extension of their legs. These athletes just look like they were born jumping, spinning, and flipping. Watching these heroes inspires you—and intimidates you at the same time.

## THE ORIGINALS

One of the first in-line skating pros to grab attention was Chris Edwards, nicknamed "Airman" for vert tricks that sent him soaring. Featured in the 1993 movie *Airborne*, starring Seth Green and Jack Black, he motivated many people to start skating. Over the years, Edwards has had four types of skates named after him, in addition to appearing in the video game *Aggressive In-line* and starting his own skate park.

Another original skater to go professional was Jaren Grob, also known as "The Monster" for his forceful style on skates. Watching him win awards at competitions like the X Games made it hard to believe that he started out as a skater in the Ringling Brothers and Barnum and Bailey circuses.

JAREN GROB THRILLS AUDIENCES WITH HIS AGGRESSIVE STYLE OF IN-LINE SKATING.

## Today's Heroes

In recent years, some of the biggest names in in-line skating have been Taig Khris, brothers Takeshi and Eito Yasutoko, Chris Haffey, and Fabiola da Silva. Khris began roller skating at the age of six and never stopped. He rode his first half-pipe at fifteen and put on his first pair of in-line skates at twenty-one. Since then, he has become one of the sport's most recognized stars and the master of the double backflip.

The Yasutoko brothers are part of what is known as the "first skate family of Japan." The boys' parents were both professional skaters, and so Takeshi and Eito learned to skate as toddlers and were competing before they became teenagers. They even had their own

TAKESHI YASUTOKO (RIGHT) ENKOURAGES HIS BROTHER EITO DURING THE 2004 X GAMES IN LOS ANGELES, CALIFORNIA.

skate park at home and practiced three or four hours every day. The brothers invented their own moves, including the double flat spin and the 1440 flat spin—four full turns! According to former **BMX** champion Jamie Bestwick, the Yasutoko brothers are the dominant vert riders in any discipline you can name.

Another powerhouse of the in-line skating world is Chris Haffey, otherwise known as "Superman" or the "Bonecrusher." He began skating at the age of two; a few of his friends who played ice hockey introduced him to aggressive skating when he was eleven.

In the beginning, Haffey mainly skated on the street, but it did not take long for him to realize that he could make a good living through winning skate contests. For years, he did just that: won virtually every major contest since 2005. In 2009 he won gold in Shanghai's X Games.

## Not for Boys Only

Although the majority of in-line skaters are male, females can excel at the sport also. Just ask Fabiola da Silva, the

FABIOLA DA SILVA IS THE PREMIER FEMALE IN-LINE SKATER.

top female pro skater in the world and multiple X Games champion (1996–2000). Fabby, as she is nicknamed, began skating at age nine and by seventeen had turned pro. She has earned over fifty medals and has performed so well in competitions that the sport introduced the "Fabiola rule," allowing women to compete in vert competitions that had previously banned them. In 2005

# A NEW WORLD'S RECORD

IN-LINE SKATERS ARE KNOWN for coming up with amazing and risky new tricks, but the activities of Dirk Auer, from Germany, may have earned the title of craziest tricks of all. First Auer put on skates and, pulled behind a motorcycle on a closed section of an express highway in Germany called the Autobahn, he hit speeds of 180 miles per hour. Next, he worked for two months to create a specially made pair of in-line skates to use for skating on a roller coaster track that was 2,822 feet long. His frames were attached to the wooden track at the Trips Drill theme park in Stuttgart, Germany. Off he went, soaring up and down; in just under 60 seconds Auer had covered a little over half a mile. As he puts it, "I was a human roller-coaster car. Nobody had ever come up with such an insane idea before!"

she astonished crowds by becoming the first woman to land the double backflip on a vert ramp.

Another female face in in-line skating is Jenna Downing from England. She is the 2008 LG Action Sports World champion and reigning World Street Champion. She has been competing since she was eight years old, and she became the youngest female in the world to turn pro—at the age of twelve.

# FIVE

# TAKING IT TO THE NEXT LEVEL

**THERE IS GOOD NEWS** when it comes to in-line skating competition. In 2009 a new organization united all the major independent skating events throughout the world. Known as the World Rolling Series, it was founded by a combination of company owners and skating legends. By linking together skaters, event organizers, retailers, and skate parks, the World Rolling Series is able to sponsor more than a hundred events in more than twenty different countries.

More good news is that if you are a great in-line skater and love doing tricks and discovering new skills, you don't have to confine yourself to local and street competitions.

## More Ways to Skate

It only seems right for in-line skaters to return to hockey, since that is where the skates got their beginning. Roller hockey is played on a dry surface rather than in an ice rink. The puck is called a biscuit and tends to have rollers on the bottom of it to help it slide across surfaces. Sticks, pads, biscuit, and of course, helmets are all you need to form a team. The USA Hockey InLine organization helps get schools and other organizations started in this sport.

SOME IN-LINE SKATERS TAKE THEIR SKILL TO THE RINK AND PLAY COMPETITIVE GAMES OF IN-LINE HOCKEY.

If you love FAST, speed skating is the sport for you. Skates are a little different—five wheels instead of four, a long wheel platform, and low-cut boots. Speed skating races can range from a 328-foot to 3.1-mile sprints all the way to relay races or ultra-long-distance runs like the one that takes place in Georgia, from Athens to Atlanta. The most common length

IF SPEED IS YOUR THING, SPEED SKATING RACES ARE THE WAY TO GO.

## FLY A KITE!

FLYING A KITE CAN be great fun, especially if on a windy day along the beach or in a grassy field. Couple that with skates and you get the brainchild of Bob Childs: kite skating. Childs decided to combine kites that could be steered with in-line skating. He built a special pair of skates with scooter wheels that he named the Wheels of Doom. Holding onto kite strings, he and other fans have found ways to be propelled across parking lots, fields, beaches, or dry lakes at speeds of up to 60 miles per hour—solely by wind power!

JOIN THE THOUSANDS WHO'VE MADE IN-LINE SKATING THEIR NUMBER ONE HOBBY!

is 12.4 miles, and skaters have been clocked going as fast as 68 miles per hour.

Be sure to check out all of the information at USA Roller Sports—it has information on every kind of skating.

If pulling on a pair of in-line skates and learning how to move faster, jump higher, spin quicker, reach farther, or flip smoother is important to you, go for it! More and more skate parks are being built across the country, and although competitions are harder to find on the national and international level, they do exist closer to home. After all, skating is for YOU, not for an award.

Put on your safety equipment, take some lessons, and get rolling. It's time to catch some air!

# GLOSSARY

**bearings** steel ball bearings housed inside the wheel hub of a skate and secured by frame and axle bolts

**BMX** the sport of bicycle motocross

**coping** the metal railing at the top of a ramp's walls

**durometer** a device used to measure the hardness of materials, including skate wheels

**flat** the bottom of a quarter- or half-pipe or open space at a skate park

**hub** the center of a wheel

**lip tricks** stunts done at the coping of a vert ramp

**lunge** a basic move that builds muscles and speed

**polyurethane** a plastic used to make strong, durable wheels and skate boot shells

**ramp** a wooden or concrete structure used to create quarter- and half-pipes and street obstacles

**street skating** for in-line skaters, making use of obstacles like those found in an urban environment

**transition** any curved surface used for skating

**vert** using a specially designed ramp with in-line skating

# FIND OUT MORE

**BOOKS**

David, Jack. *In-Line Skating*. New York: Children's Press, 2008.

Kaelberer, Angie Peterson. *Aggressive In-Line Skating*. Mankato, MN: Capstone Press, 2006.

Shafran, Michael. *Skate: Your Guide to Inline, Aggressive, Vert, Street, Roller Hockey, Speed Skating, Dance, Fitness, Training and More*. Washington, D.C.: National Geographic, 2008.

**DVD**

*The Best Inline Skating Instructions Ever!* Custom Flix, 2006.

**WEBSITES**

**Aggressive.com/Inline Skating**

www.aggressive.com

Billed as "a place for booters to hang, swap stories, pics, videos, and share random skating stuff," this site is mainly for skaters who want to connect with others.

**Be Magazine**

www.be-mag.com

An online magazine, *Be* features interviews, events, and a message board for skaters.

**International Inline Skating Association (IISA)**

www.iisa.org

This website provides helpful links to multiple resources including where to find equipment, trainers, and events. It also features news and research on the sport.

# INDEX

Page numbers in **boldface** are illustrations.

## ABOUT THE AUTHOR

**TAMRA ORR** is the author of more than 250 books for readers of all ages. A graduate of Ball State University, Orr has a degree in secondary education and English and has written thousands of national and state assessment/test questions (hers are the ones you liked best!). Currently, she lives in the Pacific Northwest with her dog, cat, husband, and three teenagers. In her fourteen spare minutes each day, she loves to read, write letters, and travel around the state of Oregon marveling at the breathtaking scenery.